East Building

National Gallery of Art

A Profile

Introduction

The idea of the East Building really goes back to Andrew Mellon. When the original gallery—the West Building as we now call it—was completed in 1941, the collection that he gave filled only five of its 135 galleries. Yet his vision of the future was such that, though he was giving a building larger than the National Gallery in London, he made it a condition of his gift that the adjoining trapezoidal plot to the east be reserved for a future addition to the Gallery. His was an extraordinary leap of the imagination very like that of George Washington and Major L'Enfant when they envisioned a great world capital rising from the muddy site of Tiber Creek.

Only thirty years later, to everyone's suprise, through the gifts and bequests of public-spirited citizens, and without compromise as to quality, the collections had outgrown the original building. Furthermore, there was inadequate space for temporary exhibitions of the size and importance appropriate to a national gallery, since the original building was modeled so closely after its counterpart in London that no space was planned for this purpose, and the only areas that we could use were entirely too restrictive. Because the Gallery's permanent collections are limited to painting, sculpture, and graphic art of the West from the late Middle Ages to the present, we needed, through our temporary exhibition program, to reach out into the many important areas beyond the scope of our own collections to give our visitors insights into the arts of other cultures and other ages throughout time and throughout the globe.

*J. Carter Brown, director, and
Paul Mellon, president of the
National Gallery*

With the normal rate of growth of the collections as the Gallery moves toward and into the twenty-first and subsequent centuries, there will be ever-increasing fields of art to anthologize. The new building was planned with this in mind, and also to provide space for future donations. Yet it was obviously impossible to construct a building large enough to house a growing collection indefinitely. The amount of land available is limited as is the attention span of our visitors. Also we have a responsibility to lend works of art from our collections to various institutions across the country. As a result we conceived the building as a place where core samplings of various aspects of the arts of the twentieth century and beyond may be displayed in galleries differing in size and scale and disjunct from one another to provide maximum flexibility.

In the intervening years since completion of the West Building, concepts of the function of a national gallery had considerably evolved. Our commitment to scholarship necessitated a major art library for the use of curatorial staff and visiting scholars. A photographic reference archive proved to be essential. The Gallery's scholarly programs have developed. For some years now we have had a professor in residence for each term, with the Mellon lecturer coming for six weeks each spring, all chosen from among the most distinguished art historians in the world. We also provide a series of fellowships to enable younger scholars to pursue research either here or abroad, often with internships at the Gallery; about a dozen are working at any given time. This led to the idea that a Center for Advanced Study in the Visual Arts should be established as an integral part of the National Gallery of Art.

Washington has among the richest and least used resources in the arts of any city in the world. The Library of Congress is virtually next door, and there are further resources in the universities of the Washington area as well as those of institutions such as the Brookings and Carnegie institutions, Dumbarton Oaks, the various branches of the Smithsonian, the Phillips Collection, the Corcoran, and many others. The collections of the Gallery itself have been far less

4

used than are those in areas of greater academic concentration. The idea of the Center seemed a natural function of the Gallery, to provide space and facilities so that scholars could work in close proximity with great works of art, surrounded with the necessary tools of scholarship, remote from the exigencies of teaching, managing theses, and of too frequent academic committee chores. It would allow them to substitute, in a sympathetic setting, actual personal contact with works of art for shadowy images on the lecture hall screen.

For these various reasons, and because all the departments of the museum had outgrown spaces available to them, the East Building became essential to the Gallery's effective operation and development. But it was also planned to provide our visitors with an aesthetic experience in addition to all its other functions. I had the impression that our architect was somewhat surprised when he found a client listing quite seriously among the programmatic requirements, along with all of the square footages and engineering tolerances, that the building had to be beautiful. In art museums we should be in the business of practicing what we preach, and we preach very strongly the sensitizing of our fellows to the best in our visual environment, and should therefore try to do this by example as well as by precept. It seemed that, if we were constructing a great new architectural space, we should seek to have it reflect the best thinking of our time, both visual thinking in architectural terms and in other branches of the visual arts. That is why we included an important group of commissioned or specially selected works in various media, to be placed in the main court and adjacent areas—these have all been donated by a group of generous citizens organized as a Collectors Committee which includes members from all parts of the country, who have followed the progress of the building with keen interest. Because of the scale of the building one could not simply shop around for existing works to match it. We have often been impressed by the successes of other periods in combining architecture with its sister arts, for example as in medieval European cathedrals or palaces of the seventeenth and

Bird's-eye view of the East and West Buildings of the National Gallery. Below, the architect of the East Building, I. M. Pei, and his associate, Leonard Jacobson

eighteenth centuries. It seemed an ideal opportunity to enlist several of the masters of today to provide examples of their works appropriate in character and in scale to the sites allotted them in the new building.

Many look at the uncompromising contemporaneity of the building and assume that it is to house only contemporary art. There are the modern works that were commissioned, and there are modern masterpieces in the various inaugural exhibitions. But the largest, *The Splendor of Dresden: Five Centuries of Art Collecting*, is entirely devoted to works of the past. It is dedicated to tracing the history of the collecting idea as it evolved in our European heritage, using a single city to illustrate that evolution. As the attitude toward collecting developed, the idea of exhibition for public instruction and public enjoyment developed as well. In many senses, the East Building of the National Gallery is, on the day of its opening, the latest stage in that developmental process.

There is an approximate chronology linking

the various opening exhibitions as one moves upward through the building from the concourse level. On the ground floor is a selection from the best of the Gallery's master drawings and water-colors, shown together for the first time, along with others which are promised gifts. On the same floor is the collection of impressionist and post-impressionist paintings left to the Gallery by Ailsa Mellon Bruce. Because of their intimate scale, it has never been possible to exhibit them since they came to the nation, but the galleries in which they are installed were designed with just this kind of scale in mind.

This year marks the two-hundredth anniversary of the death of Giovanni Battista Piranesi, one of the most imaginative artists of the western tradition. For this reason it seemed a particularly appropriate time to gather examples of the artist's early architectural etchings. A catalogue raisonné is being published in connection with the exhibition.

Also on the mezzanine and continuing on the floors above is an exhibition in three parts, which

we have called *Aspects of Twentieth-Century Art* because it does not pretend to be a survey. The first part is devoted to Picasso and cubism. Part two includes an extraordinary group of works of the fauves lent by John Hay Whitney, a trustee of the Gallery, some fascinating futurist pieces lent by Dr. and Mrs. Barnett Malbin, and a group of Giacometti sculptures, all now a part of the Gallery's collection thanks to the generosity of Mrs. Enid A. Haupt. Part three of *Aspects of Twentieth-Century Art* continues in the tower gallery on the floor above, with Matisse's "Jazz" portfolio and five from among his late cut-outs, forming probably the world's greatest collection of this aspect of his work.

Another temporary exhibition, *American Art at Mid-Century: The Subjects of the Artist*, is installed on the upper floor. It explores the work of seven Americans: six painters and a sculptor, who pursued, sometimes with an almost demonic energy, a single theme which was predominant during a highly creative part of their careers. All the works center around the middle period of our own century and were done by some of the most outstanding artists of our times. In a climactic gallery, with its skylighted ceiling raised to the maximum height of thirty-five feet, contains the Voltri sculptures by David Smith. They were created by him when he was invited by the organizers of the Spoleto Festival to go to Italy and make a piece to be shown in the Roman amphitheater nearby, and ended up by populating the ancient arena with his powerful dark bronze imagery.

In addition, there are two smaller exhibits which indicate essential activities and services, and show something of what goes on behind the scenes in the Gallery. One, on the ground level of the administrative offices and Study Center, traces the ways in which the research of scholars in various fields is translated into a form which may be understood and appreciated by the American public across the nation. The other, in the lobby of the large auditorium on the Concourse level, dramatizes the ways in which the Gallery attempts to fufill its national mandate to be of

JAMES PIPKIN

maximum possible service, not only to those who come to Washington, but also throughout the country. Audio-visual and other materials are circulated by the Gallery without charge to reach more than four thousand communities in all fifty states of the union.

Later in the inaugural year, other shows will be current. Since works on paper suffer from light and may be shown safely only for a limited time, the master drawings exhibition will be replaced by a survey of the works of one of the most delightful draftsmen of all time, the French rococo artist Fragonard, simultaneously with a companion show of the work of his friend and talented contemporary, Hubert Robert.

The Dresden exhibition will move on to New York and then to San Francisco, and be replaced with the works of an artist who occupies a most significant position in the evolution of twentieth-century art, Edvard Munch. Because there are almost no examples of his paintings in American museums, and because of the tremendous weight given to the School of Paris and the obvious

*Balthasar Permoser and Johann
Melchior Dinglinger:* Moor
Carrying a Tray of Emeralds, *1724,
Grünes Gewölbe, Dresden. Above,
Jan Vermeer:* Woman by a Window,
Reading a Letter, *c. 1658,
Gemäldegalerie Alte Meister, Dresden*

advances which took place in France during the
nineteenth and early twentieth century, Munch
has been underappreciated in this country. He
sold little during his lifetime and left the bulk of
his studio production to his native city of Oslo.
We have been fortunate in securing unprece-
dented loans from the Munch Museum, the
National Gallery of Oslo, the gallery in Bergen,
as well as other sources, to enable us to survey
the full range of his achievements on both canvas
and paper.

I. M. Pei, the architect of the East Building, is
a great admirer of the original National Gallery,
with its axes crossing at right angles, its
symmetry and clarity of plan. In designing the
new building, he projected the longitudinal axis
of the West Building, which runs down the center
of the building, through the middle of the
Rotunda and the Garden Courts, and is parallel
to Constitution Avenue and the Mall, extending
it across the intervening Plaza to bisect the East
Building's façade exactly between the towers to
culminate at the prow of the third tower. This
linking of the older building and the new by a
common axis is further strengthened by a
sensitive adjustment in height and the use of
a common material. The great interior space,
with its adjoining galleries at lower ceiling
height, recalls the system of contrasting interior
volumes in the West Building. From this point
on, however, the two buildings are markedly
different, because the East Building is also
planned to express at the same time another and
different axis, the diagonal one that parallels
Pennsylvania Avenue, thus reflecting the two
major axes of Major L'Enfant's plan for
Washington, the one from the Capitol along the
Mall toward the Washington Monument and the
Lincoln Memorial, and the other northwest from
the Capitol up Pennsylvania Avenue to the White
House. The angle at which these two axes come
together became a governing principle for the
design of the new building. One sees it in the
marble floors, in the coffers of the ceilings, in the
patterns of the space-frame above the court, in
the cross section of the piers, in the angles of the
stairs, and even in the roofs of the elevator cabs.
The building is therefore forthrightly asymmetri-

cal, even though its west façade answers directly to the long axis of the West Building. The strict geometry of the plan provides a sense of harmony, while the consistent departure from symmetry lends a sense of excitement to the experience of the building.

An essential function of a museum, other than to preserve and display works of art, is to provide visitors with a special kind of experience, one that goes further and deeper than the common-place of everyday life. In a theater this is accomplished by having us take our seats, allowing the house lights to dim, so that we can then, sitting silently in the dark, participate in what happens in the fantasy world of the brightly lit stage or screen. In a museum it happens in a different way. The museum, so often visited during work-a-day hours, must rely on its architecture to help prepare us. In the West Building, we enter into the great domed rotunda where we are surrounded by serene architecture and the sound of the splashing water of the fountain. We orient ourselves as we walk through the tall sculpture halls; there is a gradual lowering of ceiling height and size of space as we reach the rooms in which the works of art are displayed. This processional process over time gives us the sense that we are in a very special place and prepares us emotionally and psycho-logically for the experience, so that we may begin our very personal dialogues with individual works of art.

The entire plan of the West Building is governed by the precision of right angles, reflecting the volumetric world view which has prevailed in the West from Roman times until recently. Since the late Renaissance, especially in the early years of the twentieth century, our view of reality has changed. We no longer have the confidence of earlier centuries that we know all the answers. As we experimented and explored, our cosmology has become less clear, and our sense of time has changed. There are still Stone Age people living in the age of space. Our ideas of art have changed also: yesterday's artifact or utilitarian object has become today's work of art. The theory of relativity emerged at

Albrecht Dürer: A Tuft of Cowslips, *1526. Promised Gift of the Armand Hammer Foundation*

Vincent van Gogh: Harvest—The
Plain of La Crau, *c. 1888, Promised
Gift of Mr. and Mrs. Paul Mellon.
Below, Edgar Degas:* Madame
Dietz-Monnin, 1879, *National
Gallery of Art, Gift of Mrs.
Albert J. Beveridge in memory of
her aunt, Delia Spencer Field*

exactly the same time as the birth of cubism. Our world, then, is one of multiplicity and simultaneity, and our approach to it assumes not one point of reference but many, with time a significant dimension. This is reflected with great clarity in the East Building. Its plan and its spaces are no longer orthogonal but triangulate. Like the West Building, it provides a processional experience. If one enters the concourse level through the connecting link, the long tunnel is a contemplative preparation, and the clear colors of the Arp tapestry at the end invite one on into the lobby where the space explodes over one's head.

When entering from the plaza and the front exterior porch, the splayed side walls of the two west towers offer welcome, and the coffered overhang high above, shelter. The glimpses through the glass walls invite, especially when aglow with light at night. Through the revolving doors one enters a low space which is almost intimate in scale before moving out into the light-flooded court with its soaring space-

Andrea Mantegna: Bird on a Branch, *c. 1495, Andrew W. Mellon Fund. Below, Giovanni Battista Piranesi:* Sawhorse *from the* Carceri, *W. G. Russell Allen, Ailsa Mellon Bruce, Lessing J. Rosenwald, and Pepita Milmore Funds. Right, Picasso:* The Gourmet, *1901, Chester Dale Collection*

frame high above, against which is defined the hovering Calder mobile. The view ahead of trees, sculpture, tapestries, and paintings lead one imperceptibly to the right as the center of gravity of the new buildings skews southward from the axis of the old, though the latter determined the place of entrance. Again, one is in a very special place, but with a totally different atmosphere. The glass walls allow constant and instinctive orientation, but the molding of the space is varied and unpredictable, constantly changing. One can see many of the works of art from several different angles and levels. As one progresses through the central space, using stairs, bridges, escalators in any of a variety of ways, one can keep track of where one is going and where one has been. At the same time, the experience of the building and of its contents is kinetic, reflecting the world of today and tomorrow.

In all that the East Building implies as well as in all it provides, it looks to a confident and hopeful future. That future has been opened to us by the continuing partnership with the federal government which maintains the National Gallery; by the generosity of many citizens from all parts of the nation who support our efforts with gifts and donations; and, in a very special way, by the president of the Gallery, Paul Mellon, and his late sister, and the foundation which he and his sister established, the source of the funding necessary to construct the building. It seems appropriate that an idea which began with Andrew W. Mellon should have been realized by his children, in a consistent record of generosity which may well be unique in the history of philanthropy.

J. Carter Brown
Director

Henri Matisse. La Négresse,
1952-53, National Gallery of Art,
Ailsa Mellon Bruce Fund

Willem de Kooning: Woman I,
*1950-52, The Museum of Modern
Art. To the right, Alberto
Giacometti:* Walking Man II, *1960,
National Gallery of Art,
Gift of Mrs. Enid A. Haupt*

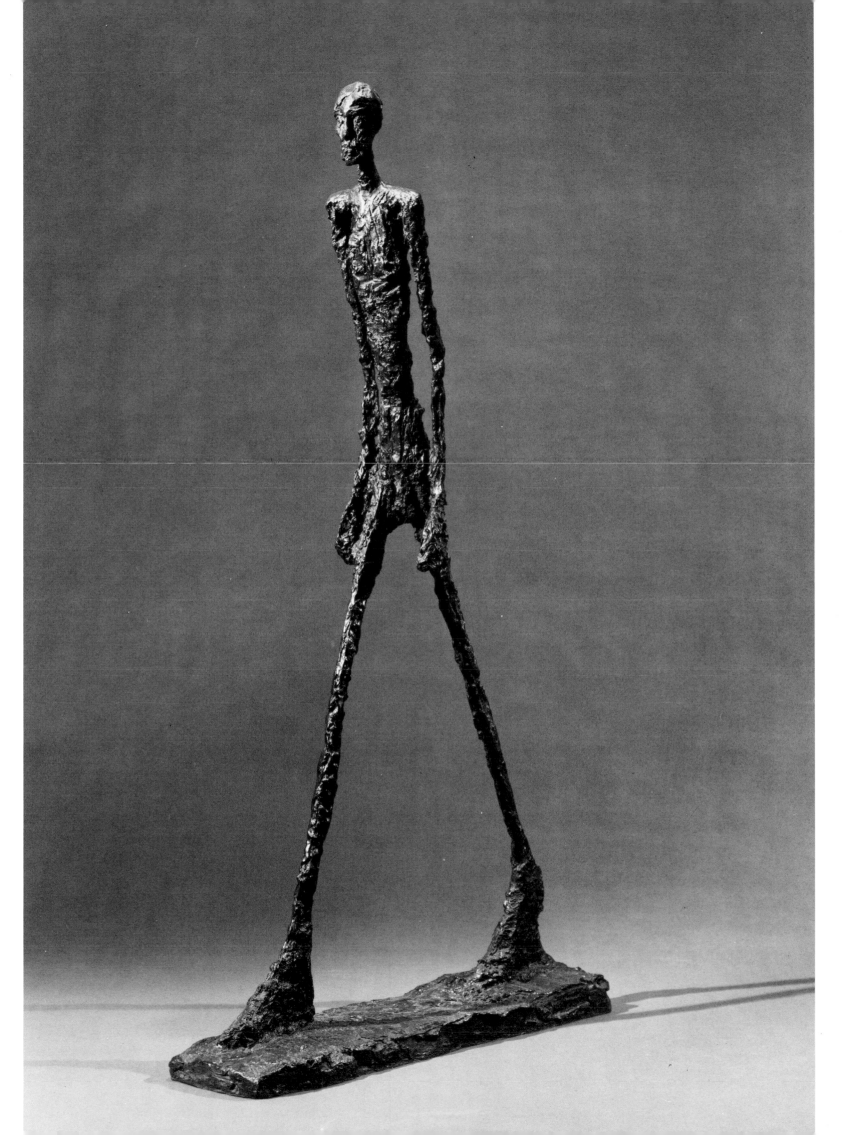

East Building

At the top of the south tower, galleries with nearly 1,500 square feet of exhibition space house special examples from the collections.

The **Upper Level** has approximately 20,000 square feet of exhibition space for the collections, plus a terrace for displaying monumental paintings and sculpture. The bridge on this level leads to escalators and the Terrace Café, which overlooks the Mall.

On the **Mezzanine** are two galleries for part of the collections, a bridge connecting two terraces for the exhibition of sculpture, a lounge and a sales area.

The **Ground Level** contains the central courtyard—the main orientation space for visitors in the East Building—a 135-foot-long sculpture pool, two galleries for exhibition of works of art, and a checkroom, information desk, and other services for visitors.

In addition to the Café/Buffet and publication sales area, the **Concourse** houses a walkway connecting the buildings in an all-weather route; a large auditorium (442 seats) for lectures, films, and other educational programs; a smaller auditorium and orientation center with a seating capacity of 90; and up to 18,000 square feet of gallery space for special exhibitions.

Services

👨 *Men's Room*

👩 *Women's Room*

🧥 *Checkroom*

❓ *Information*

📞 *Telephone*

♿ *Facilities for the Handicapped*

🛍 *Sales Shop*

⊠ *Elevator*

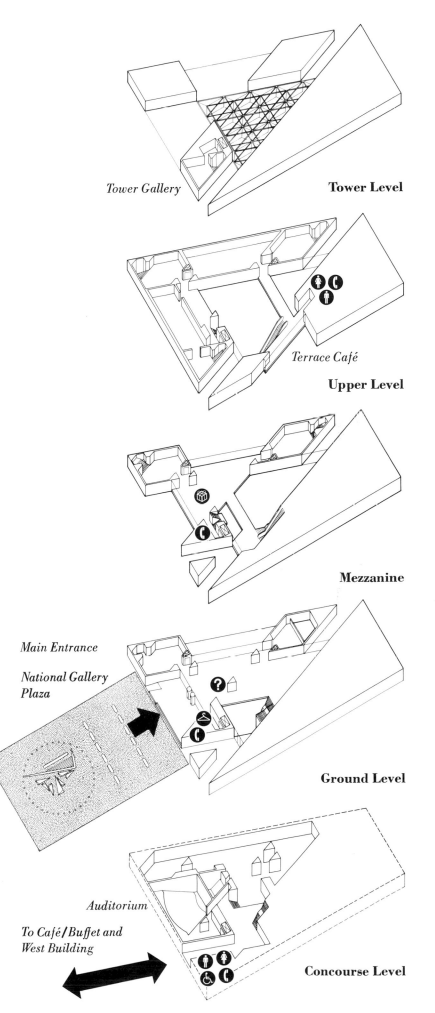

Tower Gallery   **Tower Level**

Terrace Café

Upper Level

Mezzanine

Main Entrance

National Gallery Plaza

Ground Level

Auditorium

To Café/Buffet and West Building

Concourse Level

Nolde,

The Commissioned and Specially Selected Works

The completion of the East Building marks the beginning of a new chapter in the history of the National Gallery. The opportunities it offers for observation and study, for humanistic and scientific research, in almost every aspect of the visual arts, adds a new dimension to the capacity of the Gallery to serve a growing public with an increasing interest in the arts, from the casual visitor to the most experienced scholar. In the dramatic and austere forms of its architecture, with its varied interior spaces, it provides a sympathetic environment for the display of exhibitions of any size or character. From the moment one enters the East Building, its exciting vistas and soaring spaces, reminiscent of those seen in the Piranesi prints, also on display, create a sense of adventure and invite our exploration. Like all successful buildings designed for public use, it is truly complete only when thronged with others like ourselves, who, by entering, embark on a personal voyage of discovery.

But there is more in the East Building complex than meets the eye. Out of sight below the ground are the receiving, storage, staging, and other supportive facilities, and shops necessary for packing, unpacking, and installation of exhibitions of all kinds. There are also, in another location, completely equipped laboratories for the examination and conservation of works of art in every medium.

Behind the scenes are the curatorial and administrative offices, as well as the Center for Advanced Study in the Visual Arts. In the Center, scholars from around the world will work close to the library, photographic archive, and computerized art historical information so essential to their research. There are also the headquarters of the department of education which carries out the Gallery's function of providing a learning experience, not only to those visiting the museum, but also, through its nationwide extension programs which now serve more than two and a half million people.

Emil Nolde: Head of Christ, *1909, National Gallery of Art, William Nelson Cromwell Fund*

Henry Moore

Knife Edge Mirror Two Piece, 1977/1978
Gift of the Morris and Gwendolyn Cafritz
Foundation

The immense bronze sculpture in the plaza is
an introduction to the group of outstanding
examples of the arts of today to be seen in the
new East Building. It is by Henry Moore, one of
the acknowledged masters of our time and
shows his preoccupation with organic form and
natural texture. In his studio set among the
rolling fields of Hertfordshire, twenty-five miles
north of London, surrounded by the elements
of nature which have done so much to shape his
art, he planned the monumental sculpture
especially for the place it now occupies. Like the
piece he produced for Lincoln Center fifteen
years earlier, it may be seen from many points
of view. Both are part of a group of works
which are variations on a theme. "In doing this
series," he recalled, "it came naturally . . .
that I made it in two pieces. . . . Between them I
am trying to make a kind of mixture of the
human figure and of landscape." Speaking of
the Washington bronze he remarked, "As you
move around it, the two parts overlap or they
open up and there's a space between. Sculpture
is like a journey. You have a different view
when you return." With the change in the time
of day and in the weather, and with the movement of the viewer, the sculpture changes also,
enlivened by light and shade, by rain and snow,
like the forms in nature which it echoes while
remaining unmistakably a work of man. "What
really counts," Moore said, "is the vision it
expresses."

*Above, Henry Moore in his studio
in England. Below left, the artist
with J. Carter Brown, director of
the National Gallery. Below right,
bronze casting of* Knife Edge Mirror
Two Piece *model*

After Jean Arp

Variation on "Aubette," tapestry, 1976,
National Gallery of Art,
Gift of the Collectors Committee

At the concourse level, at the end of the tunnel
with the moving sidewalk, is a tapestry after a
mural design by Jean Arp. An Alsatian, he lived
most of his life in Paris, after having exhibited
with the Blue Rider group in Munich in 1912,
and produced painting, poetry, and sculpture
with the dadaists in Zurich from 1916 to 1919.
His work was included in the first surrealist
exhibition in Paris in 1924, and during subsequent years he gained an international reputa-
tion both as a sculptor and a painter, whose
works are often informed with a spirit of
playfulness and sly humor. The design for the
tapestry is taken from a mural he painted in the
1920s in the basement nightclub of an ancient
building in Strasbourg called the Aubette. For
three centuries the building had been used as

a barracks and armory. The name comes from the French word for dawn, *aube*, because military life started at the crack of dawn. It was later made over into several restaurants, bars, and a nightclub. Though the painting was almost destroyed in a subsequent remodelling, Arp made a silkscreen print of the design in 1959. He had intended that it be made into a tapestry, but it was not woven until after his death in 1966, when the National Gallery commissioned the work specially for the East Building, to be made in Aubusson, France. The two yellow, mushroomlike forms are based on his studies of female heads with luxuriant hair but can also suggest soft-edged arrows pointing the way upstairs to the rear of the nightclub. The organic shapes with curving contours, related to the

style of both Calder and Miró, are typical of Arp, both in painting and sculpture, as is the palette of fresh, clear color. *Oriforme*, an eight-foot stainless steel abstraction fabricated in 1977 from a small maquette, or model, made by the artist probably in the early sixties, displays the same amoebic form in three dimensions that appears in his paintings and in the tapestry. It may be seen on the south side of the East Building.

Alexander Calder

Untitled, 1976
Gift of the Collectors Committee

One of the first things seen on entering the main courtyard is the mobile by Alexander Calder silhouetted overhead against the glass roof, a sequence of linked free-form plates in red, blue, and black, suspended high above. Calder's father and grandfather were both distinguished sculptors. The latter created the colossal William Penn which crowns the dome of Philadelphia's City Hall. His grandson, however, explored new directions. Trained as an engineer, and endowed with a vivid fancy and a sense of play, he created marvelous toy circuses which were the joy of both his artist friends and their children. He was fascinated with the surrealist style of Miró and, like Henry Moore, was acutely aware of natural form. Both influences are reflected in this work whose elements move like leafy branches in response to gentle currents of air, so nicely calculated is their balance. Their contrast with the strict triangular geometry of the space-frame above emphasizes the organic quality of the concept.

Calder was a pioneer in experimenting with kinetic sculpture, with its added dimension of movement. He made pieces to be driven by motors and hand-turned cranks but settled on the natural power of the wind as the ideal motivating force. His ability to handle compositions of tremendous size—this has a width of eighty-six feet—is apparent not only here but also in his "stabiles," a word coined by the artist Jean Arp, stationary sculptures in painted steel plate, making him perhaps the leading American sculptor of his generation to work with consistent success at a very large scale. To lighten the weight of this construction, the aluminum interiors of the floating forms are honeycombed. This aerospace technique, worked out by Paul Matisse of Cambridge, Massachusetts, must have appealed to Calder because of his early engineering training. Calder designed the piece for the space it now occupies and enlivens, and approved its final components the week before his death. Earlier, when asked to title it, he replied, "You don't name a baby until it's born," so his last major work of art, and one of his largest mobiles, remains untitled.

*Assembling the Alexander Calder
mobile before hanging in the central
courtyard of the East Building.
Large photograph at upper left,
J. Carter Brown, director and Paul
Mellon, president of the National
Gallery of Art. Lower left, the
artist gives final approval of
construction plans for his mobile*

33

F. CATALAROCA

F. CATALAROCA

Joan Miró

Femme, 1977
Gift of the Collectors Committee
and George L. Erion

Joan Miró, like Picasso, came from Barcelona, where he was born in 1893, in the northeastern part of Spain known as Catalonia. Like Arp, he became a leading surrealist, a sculptor as well as a painter, whose works have been exhibited in Europe, the Americas, Japan, and elsewhere. An oil painting entitled *Femme* (woman), a gift to the Gallery by Mr. Erion, was the model for the tapestry hanging at the far end of the main court. Woven in Spain of New Zealand wool by Josep Royo in his studio in Tarragona, not far from Miró's farm, in 1977, it is a bold translation of Miró's composition into another medium and at a far larger scale, until, with its thick and varied texture, it becomes almost a bas-relief in fabric. The spots and spatters in the background of the painting become yarn clusters. In a pose that suggests a ponderous dance, the massive yet buoyant figure in brilliant blue, red, green, and yellow is defined by black. As in all the artist's works an intense vigor is expressed by means of both form and color. Miró's energy and fancy are qualities he shares with his older country-man, Picasso, though the style in which he expresses them is uniquely his own.

Isamu Noguchi

Great Rock of Inner Seeking, 1975
Anonymous gift

Toward the far end of the courtyard stands the
tall upright stone sculpture by Isamu Noguchi,
an American of mixed Japanese and American
descent who was born in Los Angeles in 1904 and
spent twelve of his first fourteen years in
Chigasaki, a Japanese village by the sea, where
he had a year's apprenticeship to a cabinetmaker.
After he returned to the United States he was
confirmed in his determination to become a
sculptor by seeing in New York a show of the
work of the pioneer modernist, the Romanian
Constantin Brancusi, in 1926. "I was transfixed
by his vision," he recalled. His inborn feeling of
identification with the natural world fostered by
his early years in Japan, emerged powerfully in
his own work under the influence of Brancusi,
whom he assisted as a stonecutter in Paris while
on a Guggenheim fellowship. The title of the
Gallery's piece, *Great Rock of Inner Seeking*, has
overtones of traditional Japanese garden art and
of Zen Buddhist contemplation. The man-made
drill holes and the marks of the artist's chisel,
"the direct contact of man and matter," he
called them, contrast with the natural grain and
weathered textures of the granite and record the
stages of its creation from the quarry through
the sculptor's studio. The simple geometry of the
smooth base emphasizes its morphological form
and textural variations. Both its size—it is twelve
feet high and weighs eight and a half tons—and
its material give it a feeling of the primeval and
the timeless. An artist of extraordinary versa-
tility, Noguchi designed the well-known Akari
lanterns, stage sets for Martha Graham's dance
company, playgrounds for children, and entire
environments like Detroit's Civic Center Plaza,
complete with landscaping and sculpture.

Anthony Caro

National Gallery Ledge Piece, 1978
Gift of the Collectors Committee

Anthony Caro was born in London in 1924,
studied art there, and then for some years was
an assistant to Henry Moore, during which time
he worked on a number of Moore's major
projects. While teaching at St. Martin's in
London he became increasingly recognized as a
leader in contemporary developments in sculpture. In 1963 he taught at Bennington, Vermont,
and while in the United States, met the American
sculptor, David Smith, whose work he greatly
admired. Like Smith, Caro turned to cut and
welded steel as the medium best suited to his
vigorous and personal style, as may be seen in
the work he carried out for the Gallery. The
strips of straight and tautly curved members are
welded together in an arrangement bristling with
energy and restlessly involved in the surrounding
space, creating a dynamic and centrifugal composition, which he improvised for the unusual
placement over the door from the main court into
the further part of the building housing the
library, the Center for Advanced Study in the
Visual Arts, the graphics collection, and the
curatorial and other offices.

David Smith

Circle I, Circle II, Circle III, 1962
Ailsa Mellon Bruce Fund

Near his studio at Bolton Landing, New York,
David Smith placed these three pieces in the open
air, so that he clearly envisioned them in a spaci-
ous setting like that which has been planned for
them in the new East Building. Smith started out
as a painter but made his mark as a sculptor, so
this group combines both interests. Differences in
arrangement, size, and color provide variety
within the geometric unity resulting from their
sharing a common form. Broken into three units,
the sculpture keeps yielding a broad variety of
experiences as the viewer moves past it; at one
point it is possible to line up the three circles as if
looking down the barrel of a gun. Smith was an
outstanding exponent of what has been called the
Primary Structure movement, which comprises
works both simple in form and of a large enough
scale to relate them to architecture, because they
create their own environment by their presence.
Smith always fabricated his own pieces instead of
making either detailed drawings or a small model
to be carried out and enlarged by others, as is the
case with many sculptors who work at a large
scale today. Consequently the finish, and, in this
case, the color are entirely within the artist's
personal control. The result is a greater individ-
uality despite the rather anonymous quality of
the simple but forceful shapes. The materials and
the forms Smith used reflect his awareness of the
impersonal and technological character of
today's highly industrialized world.

41

James Rosati

Untitled, 1978
Gift of the Collectors Committee

Rosati had a musical career before turning to
sculpture. He played the violin with the Pitts-
burgh String Symphony in the twenties and took
up sculpture, working under the WPA program,
in the thirties. In 1944 he moved to New York
where he met David Smith, whose influence on
his development was significant. He has taught at
the Pratt Institute and Cooper Union in New
York and has been a visiting professor at both
Dartmouth and Yale. His sculptures are in major
collections throughout the country. Though he
has worked in wood and marble, metal—the most
widely used material for sculpture today—is the
appropriate medium with which to carry out the
large near-prismatic forms of this piece. It is an
enlargement of a smaller sculpture, a gift to the
Gallery in memory of the great curator and art
historian William Seitz, increased to its present
scale to suit the position that it now occupies.
It is painted white so that the shadows it casts on
itself become a part of the total effect, and the
play of light and shade further enlivens its
planar surfaces.

Robert Motherwell

Reconciliation Elegy, 1978
Gift of the Collectors Committee

Motherwell, an American painter and writer, was one of the group of artists, often called the New York School, who led the abstract expressionist movement which emerged during the fifties and rapidly won worldwide recognition. Abstract expressionism combines elements of surrealism —an often nonrepresentational style influenced by the psychological theories of Freud and the life of the unconscious and of dreams—and expressionism which, by the use of formal distortion, a bold and often unnaturalistic use of color, and slashing brushwork, endeavored to convey emotional force. Entitled *Reconciliation Elegy*, Motherwell's mural-sized canvas is the latest in a long series begun in 1948 reflecting the horror and destruction of the Spanish civil war, the source also of Picasso's famous *Guernica*, another mural-sized painting, of 1937, protesting the lethal bombing of an undefended village. Motherwell's paintings are less dramatic and more elegiac. The brooding black shapes looming against a light ground suggest a mood of anguish and a sense of doom, of the awareness and imminence of death. Its stark forms also reflect the rigor and austerity which characterize much of Spanish life and history. Motherwell has said that his Elegies are not specifically political, but are rather "general metaphors of the contrast between life and death, and their interrelation." In this last and largest of them, the dynamism of the black shapes contrasts with the delicate color beneath to add a trace of enlivening energy to the severity which pervades the earlier works of the series.

ROBERT BIGELOW

44

Alexander Liberman

Adam, 1970
Lent by the Storm King Art Center

Liberman has turned his hand to many things during his long career, which includes being an editor, writer, painter, photographer, and sculptor. His works have been exhibited regularly and are in museum collections both here and abroad. An exhibition of his large-scale work at Storm King, which is north of New York City on the Hudson River, in the summer of 1977 elicited highly favorable reviews, and the growing recognition that despite the variety of other gifts, the artist has become recognized as a major sculptural talent of our time. *Adam* was last shown in Washington in 1970, the year in which he created it, as a part of the retrospective exhibition of his paintings and sculpture at the Corcoran Gallery. Its circular form and bright color set up a vibrant contrast with the geometry of the building, with its one triangular component offering a wry comment on the architecture's primary theme. Though he has done work of various sizes, he is best known as a sculptor of very large pieces such as this, fabricated in steel and painted, which measures 28′ 6″ x 29′ 6″ x 24′ 6″. Among his books are *Greece, Gods and Art*, and *The Artist in His Studio*. This sculpture is on loan for the period of one year, occupying a platform along the north façade that can be used for changing sculptural displays.

First Year Inaugural Exhibitions

The Splendor of Dresden:
Five Centuries of Art Collecting

Dresden has been renowned for centuries as a vital center of the arts. Despite wars and social upheavals, the city enjoyed a cultural continuity from the sixteenth century to the Second World War and the partition of Germany. As the capital of the independent duchy of Saxony, it was influenced by the ideas of the Renaissance brought north from Italy, and under its rulers, powerful as hereditary electors of the Holy Roman Emperors, the city on the Elbe became a properous center of trade. To display both his status and his cultural interests, Augustus I began in 1650 to collect for his *Kunstkammer*, a room in the electoral palace which became crowded with all sorts of objects of art and curiosity, with a special emphasis on tools and mechanical contrivances reflecting Dresden's leadership in manufacturing and skilled crafts.

It was in the eighteenth century, however, that Dresden became a brilliant cultural center under the rule of two princes of extraordinary vision and determination, Augustus the Strong (1670-

49

1733) and his son, Augustus III (1696-1763), both of whom were also elected kings of Poland. During this period Dresden became an ideal baroque city of ordered vistas and handsome avenues, a city of wealth and magnificence which was itself a work of art, best known to us today through the fascinating views painted in the 1740s by the Venetian Bernardo Bellotto, who was court painter to Augustus II.

In Bellotto's paintings we can see the extra-ordinarily handsome architectural composition for which the city was world famous, with the bulbous-topped spire of the Catholic *Hofkirche* by the Roman architect Gaetano Chiaveri, and the tall dome of Georg Bahr's Protestant *Frauenkirche* rising high above a skyline animated by sculpture and a variety of architectural features. Most evocative of the spirit of animation and gaiety of Dresden during its heyday, however, is the remarkable complex of pavilions and galleries known as the *Zwinger*, designed by Matthäus Daniel Pöppelmann. The northeastern side was built in large part between 1709 and 1717, but the southwestern side was not completed until 1847-1849 with the Picture Gallery designed by Gottfried Semper. Though most of this was totally destroyed by Allied bombing in 1945, the extraordinary art collections, assembled over a period of five centuries, survived.

Far left: Dragoon Vase, *K'ang Hsi period, c. 1700. Above left:* Porcelain Armorial Plate, *Meissen. Below left: Johann Kirchner (?):* Whippet and Bulldog Fighting, *porcelain, Meissen, c. 1732. Top right: Johann Kändler (?):* The Grand Turk, *porcelain, Meissen, 1741-1742. Bottom right,* Porcelain Vase. *All from the Porzellansammlung, Dresden.*

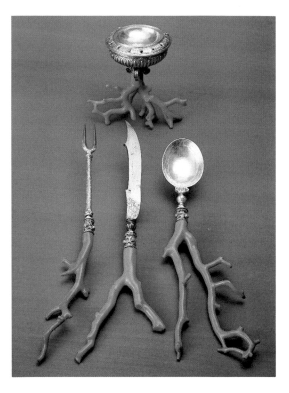

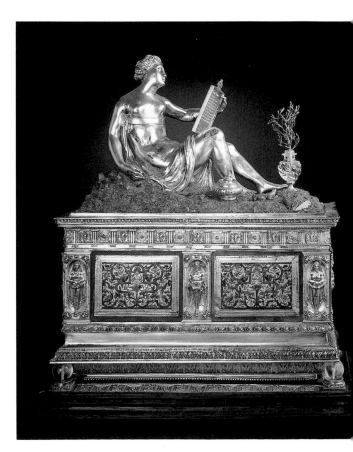

Above: Medal of the Order of the Golden Fleece, *from the rose diamond garniture of the Saxon crown treasure, late 18th century. Above near right:* Silver-gilt Table Service with Coral Handles, *Genoa, 1579. Above right:* Joshua and Caleb, *gold with enamel and jewels, early 18th century, Dresden. Above, far right:* Covered Cup Surmounted by a Man on a Rearing Horse, *gold. Near right: Wenzel Jamnitzer:* Box for Writing Utensils, *Nuremberg, 1562, gold with enamel, rock crystal, and ebony. Far right:* Leaping Unicorn, *bronze 1570-1580, Augsburg. All from the Grünes Gewölbe, Dresden.*

Above right: Eagle-Shaped Helmet, *worn by the Danish king on his state visit to Dresden in 1709. Below left:* Turkish Mace and Sword, *studded with turquoise and rubies. Below right:* Parade Helmet, *1599, Augsburg. Farther right:* Rapier and Dagger with Watches in the Pommels, *c. 1610. Far right above:* Revolver, *c. 1590, Augsburg, and* Powder Flask, *early seventeenth century. Far right below:* Shield, *c. 1600, Augsburg. All from the Historisches Museum, Dresden.*

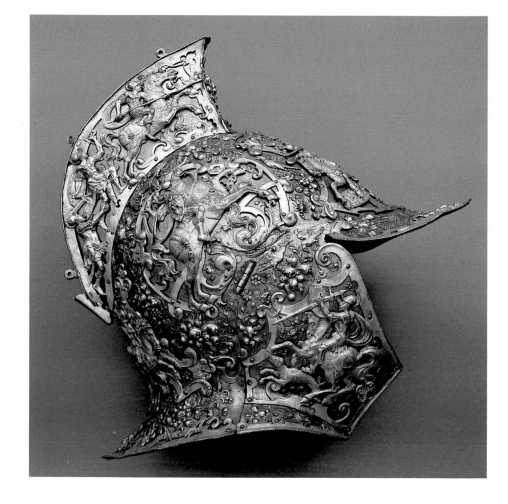

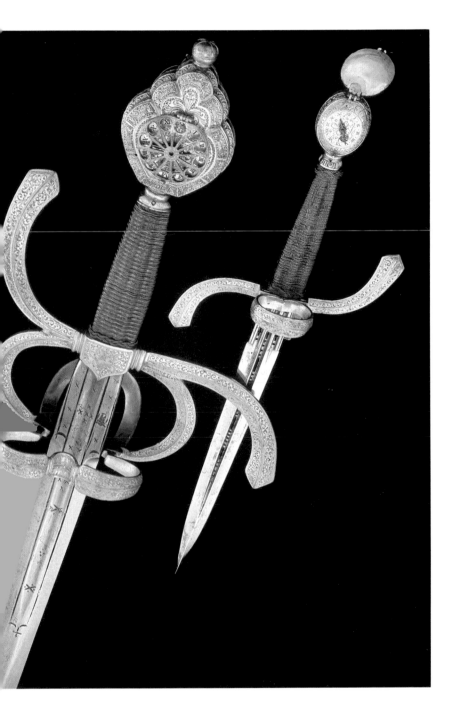

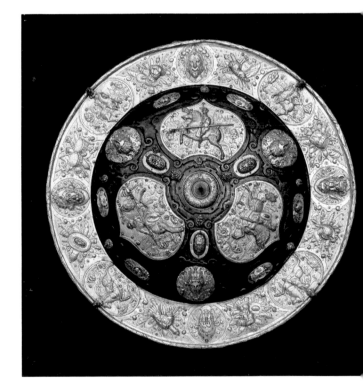

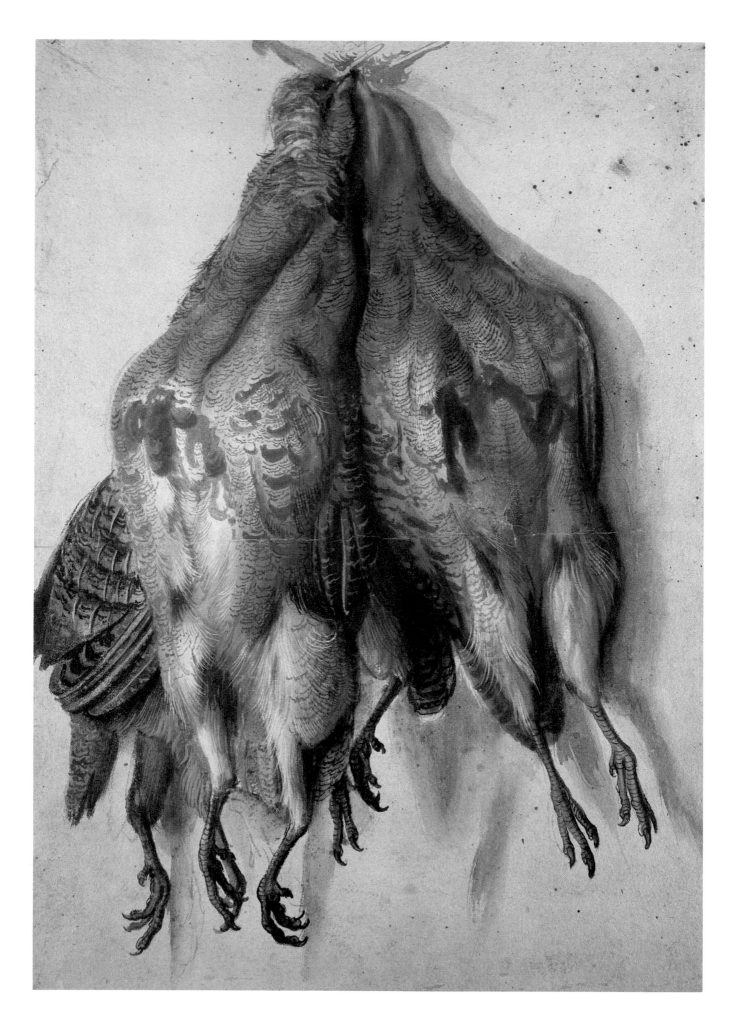

Left: Lucas Cranach the Elder:
Four Dead Partridges, *c. 1530,*
watercolor, Kupferstichkabinett.
Right: Albrecht Dürer: Portrait of
Bernhard von Reesen. *Center: Lucas*
Cranach the Elder: Portrait of
Duke Heinrich the Pious, *1514. The*
last two from the Gemäldegalerie
Alte Meister.

Near right: Peter Paul Rubens:
Mercury and Argus, *c. 1638. Below:*
Nicholas Poussin: The Realm of
Flora, *1630-1631. Far right:*
Bernardo Strozzi: Female Musician
with a Viola da Gamba, *c. 1635. All*
from the Gemäldegalerie Alte
Meister, Dresden.

Before the bombardment they had been carried off to the Soviet Union where they stayed for a quarter of a century when the greater part of them was finally returned. Subsequently they were reorganized and installed in nine State Museums by the government of the German Democratic Republic.

The selection of roughly seven hundred objects for this exhibition was made, not on the basis of artistic distinction alone, but as a sampling to provide the visitor to the exhibition with a grasp of their extraordinarily varied character, including arms and armor, clocks and instruments, porcelains and goldsmithwork, furniture and jewels, antiquities and sculpture in bronze and marble, drawings and prints, and paintings from the Renaissance on. The installations reflect the settings originally planned for them, thus suggesting their history and evolution, and illustrating the great European tradition of princely collecting, a function which our art museums of today endeavor to continue.

Below: Caspar David Friedrich:
Two Men Contemplating the Moon,
*1819/1820. Right: Karl Schmidt-
Rottluff:* Woman's Head with Mask,
*1912. Both from the Gemäldegalerie
Neue Meister, Dresden.*

American Art at Mid-Century:
The Subjects of the Artist

Left: Robert Motherwell: Elegy to the Spanish Republic, No. 34, *1953-1954, Albright-Knox Art Gallery, Buffalo, New York, Gift of Seymour H. Knox. Lower left: members of the staff of the Gallery's Design and Installation Department. Lower right: Jackson Pollock:* Lavender Mist, *1950, National Gallery of Art, Ailsa Mellon Bruce Fund*

This exhibition centers on the middle period of our own century and includes several of the most outstanding artists of our times. The first section, to the east, contains the 1950 drip paintings of Jackson Pollock, done in the space of a few months, which altered the course of Western art by developing a way of painting that did not involve the brushstroke.

The next section is devoted to the *Elegies on the Spanish Republic* by Robert Motherwell, which display a powerful visual vocabulary. Then there are the *Stations of the Cross* by Barnett Newman which have been exhibited only twice before. A group of the late paintings by Mark Rothko is next, one of which has never been shown. Following is the *Plow and the Song* series by Arshile Gorky, who combined the

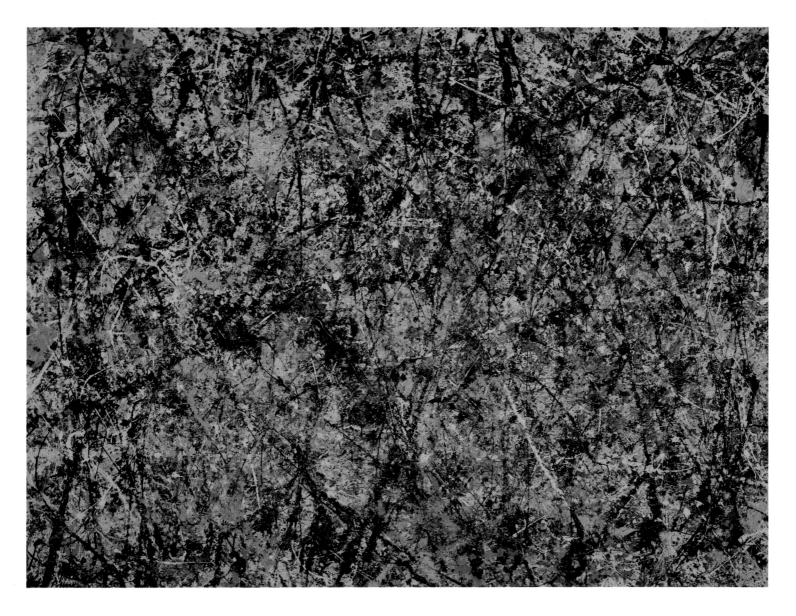

experiments of European surrealism with his own feeling for his Armenian folk heritage. Next is the original set of six paintings entitled *Woman* by Willem de Kooning, reassembled for the occasion, one from the National Gallery of Australia, another from Teheran's new museum.

In the final gallery of the exhibition, with its ceiling raised to the maximum height of thirty-five feet, are the Voltri sculptures by David Smith. Inspired by the classical imagery around him in central Italy, he produced piece after piece. This is the first time so many of them have been reassembled. The installation recreates the spirit of their original setting in an ancient amphitheater, in daylight, in the open air.

Left: Arshile Gorky: The Plow and
the Song, *1947, Allen Memorial Art
Museum, Oberlin College, R.T.
Miller, Jr. Fund. Right: Arshile
Gorky:* The Plow and the Song, *1946,
Art Institute of Chicago, Mr. and
Mrs. Lewis Larned Coburn Fund*

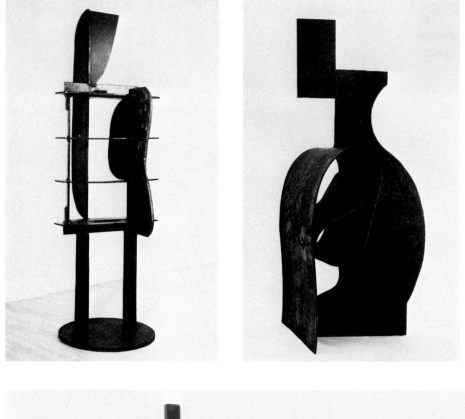

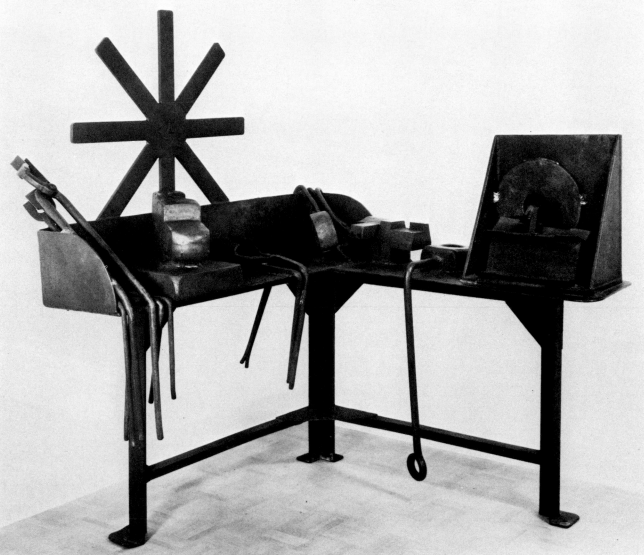

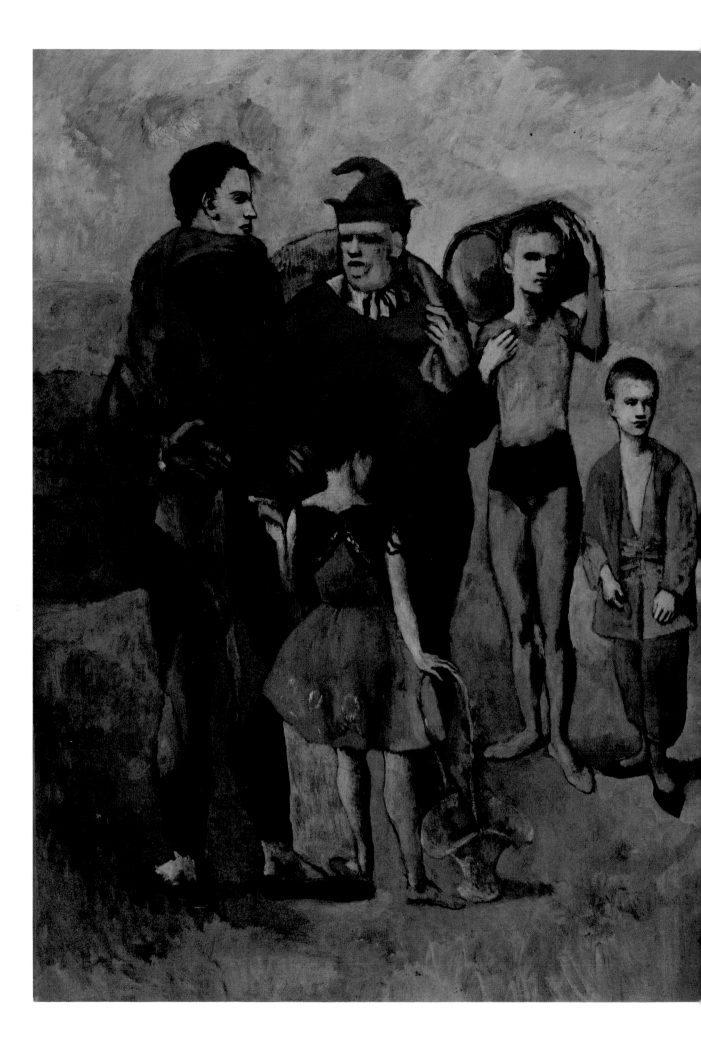

Starting on the mezzanine and continuing on the floors above, is an exhibition in three parts. The first is devoted to Picasso and the beginning of cubism, while the second shows examples of European painting and sculpture mostly before the Second World War, including the German expressionist, Beckmann, the moving early sculptures of Lehmbruck, and those of Brancusi, landmarks in the evolution of modern art. Among others represented are the orphist, Delaunay; the constructivists, Puni and Pevsner; and Arp, Miró, and other surrealists. The final gallery of this section contains the work of two outstanding English artists, Ben Nicholson and Henry Moore. Part three of *Aspects of Twentieth-Century Art* continues in the tower gallery on the floor above with the mural-sized cut-outs of Matisse and his portfolio, *Jazz.*

Left: Pablo Picasso: Family of Saltimbanques, *1905, National Gallery of Art, Chester Dale Collection. Right: Pablo Picasso:* Lady with a Fan, *1905, National Gallery of Art, Gift of the W. Averell Harriman Foundation in memory of Marie N. Harriman*

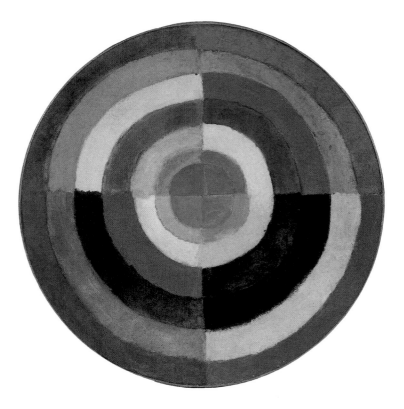

Left top: Robert Delaunay: Disc,
1912, Lent by Mr. and Mrs. Burton
Tremaine, Meriden, Connecticut.
Left below: Georges Braque: The
Harbor of La Ciotat, *1907,*
Collection of Mr. and Mrs. John
Hay Whitney. Right: Joan Miró:
Personage: The Brothers Fratellini,
1927, Collection of Dr. and Mrs.
Barnett Malbin

Left top: Maurice de Vlaminck:
Tugboat on the Seine, Chatou,
1906, Collection of Mr. and Mrs.
John Hay Whitney. Left bottom:
Umberto Boccioni: The Street
Pavers, *1911, Collection of Dr. and*
Mrs. Barnett Malbin. Right: Gino
Severini: Sea-Dancer; Dancer
Beside the Sea, *1913-1914, Collection*
of Dr. and Mrs. Barnett Malbin

Left: Henri Matisse: Checker Players, *1923, Collection of Mr. and Mrs. Paul Mellon. Right: Henri Matisse:* Open Window, Collioure, *1905, Collection of Mr. and Mrs. John Hay Whitney*

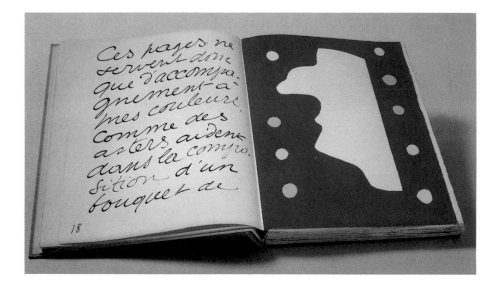

Examples of page layouts from Henri Matisse's Jazz portfolios. One portfolio is from the Collection of Mr. and Mrs. Paul Mellon and the other from the Collection of Mr. and Mrs. Andrew S. Keck

Giovanni Battista Piranesi (1720-1778), an Italian architect, became famous as an etcher whose visual records of eighteenth-century Rome are not only artistically excellent but also provide an extraordinary record, though interpreted with an intensely personal vision. His early works, done just after he left Venice for Rome, from about 1740 to 1750, are particularly admired because they are drawn with what one critic has called "the ragged brilliance that made Venice the school of etching of the eighteenth century." Among these are the four *Grotteschi* and the famous *Carceri*, or prisons. Both are full of fantasy, but the prisons are especially impressive in their gloomy vastness, with curious and massive vaulted architecture, colossal stairways, huge chains, and odd machines, all looking as if they had been created by a race of giants in some remote past. These extraordinary prints are shown along with drawings, both by Piranesi himself and by others whose work influenced him as his vigorous style evolved. Prints, drawings, and related objects have been assembled from Europe and America to give the most complete possible documentation of the artist's important early work.

Lower right: Giovanni Battista Piranesi: Carceri: The Pier with a Lamp (plate XV, 2nd edition), National Gallery of Art, W. G. Russell Allen, Ailsa Mellon Bruce, Lessing J. Rosenwald, and Pepita Milmore Funds. Lower left: Giovanni Battista Piranesi: Carceri: The Gothic Arch (plate XIV, 2nd edition), Collection of Princeton University Library. Upper right: Giovanni Battista Piranesi: Parte di ampio magnifico Porto, Collection of The New York Public Library, Prints Division. Upper left: Giovanni Battista Piranesi: Prima Parte: Ponte magnifico (plate V, 1st issue). National Gallery of Art, Ailsa Mellon Bruce Fund

For the first time all the outstanding old master drawings and watercolors from the Gallery's collection are displayed together, providing a panorama of draftmanship from the twelfth century to the Second World War. Though there are examples of the work of such famous Americans as Winslow Homer and a few of the classic moderns, the majority is European. In forming the collection quality was the only consideration, so there was no attempt to complete a chronological sequence, yet many of the various movements and schools which flourished throughout the long time span are represented. Though many drawings and water-colors are finished works of art, others record a fleeting glimpse, a visual impression, or the emergence of an idea and consequently are almost fragmentary. As a result, they engage our imagination, give us an insight into the creative process, and show the range possible within the medium.

Upper left: Henri Matisse:
Young Girl with Long Hair, *1926,*
National Gallery of Art, Lessing J.
Rosenwald Collection. Lower left:
Peter Breugel the Elder: Landscape
with the Penitence of St. Jerome,
1553, National Gallery of Art,
Ailsa Mellon Bruce Fund. Right:
Albrecht Dürer: Oriental Ruler on
his Throne, *c. 1495, National Gallery*
of Art, Ailsa Mellon Bruce Fund

Because of their intimate scale, it has never
before been possible to exhibit this collection
properly until the completion of the East
Building with its remarkable capacity to lend
itself to the display of all sizes and kinds of art.
It is a particularly personal collection, represent-
ing those artists whom Mrs. Bruce most liked
and admired. The exhibition includes both
impressionists and post-impressionists at a
superb level of quality and evidences not only
her taste and knowledge but also, because these
are the paintings she chose to live with, her
enjoyment and love of art.

Upper left: Claude Monet: Ships
Riding on the Seine at Rouen,
*1872, National Gallery of Art,
Ailsa Mellon Bruce Collection.
Lower left: Pierre Bonnard:* Two
Dogs in a Deserted Street, *c. 1893,
National Gallery of Art, Ailsa Mellon
Bruce Collection. Right: Edouard
Vuillard:* Child Wearing a Red Scarf,
*c. 1891, National Gallery of Art,
Ailsa Mellon Bruce Collection*

Following *The Splendor of Dresden*, is the first major exhibition of the 1978-79 season, showing with great fullness of detail the development of this important but comparatively little-known artist. Though there are a considerable number of his graphic works in American collections, there are almost no paintings. He sold few during his lifetime, and left almost everything to his native city of Oslo. It is the cooperative generosity of the National Gallery of Oslo, and of other collections in Norway, both public and private, that made the exhibition possible.

Not only the social unrest and conflicts of his times, but also his own tortured life formed his style and dictated the themes—love, despair, and illness—which constantly recur throughout his work. The fated yet often almost volcanic quality of his emotional life lent an emotive charge to everything he produced. His first print show is recreated as a part of the exhibition. An early unpublished notebook which comprises his own poetry and his artistic credo is on view. There is also another exhibition within the exhibition, made up of thirty or so self-portraits which span the entire length of his career and reveal his inner life with a soul-searching completeness rare in the history of art.

Left: Edvard Munch: Two Women on the Shore, c. 1910, National Gallery of Art, Print Purchase Fund (Lessing J. Rosenwald) and Ailsa Mellon Bruce Fund. Right: Central court near completion of the Center for Advanced Studies of the Visual Arts

Behind the Scenes at the National Gallery of Art

This exhibit is designed to give some indication of on-going and behind-the-scenes activities of the Gallery. It shows how the Gallery fulfills its national mandate of being of maximum service, not just to the national audience which visits Washington, but to the far larger audience across the country. The audio-visual materials which are prepared and circulated free of charge by the Gallery staff reach more than four thousand communities in all fifty states.

Located on the way to the library reading room of the Center for Advanced Study of the Visual Arts, it traces the ways in which scholarship, historical research, and scientific investigation are translated into a form which is meaningful and informative to the Gallery's wide and varied audience. By concentrating on a single painting in the collection, the portrait of *Ginevra de' Benci* by Leonardo da Vinci, the exhibit shows how virtually all the departments and branches of the Gallery combine in this multifaceted and vitally important process.

Drawings by Fragonard and Robert

After the Master Drawings exhibition, the graphic work of two outstanding French artists will share the same galleries. Jean-Honoré Fragonard (1732-1806) and his friend Hubert Robert (1733-1808) were among the last of the distinguished eighteenth-century French masters. Both lived through the French Revolution, though there is no trace of its devastating disruption and violence in their work. Fragonard gained great fame for his paintings of scenes of gallantry, while Robert, an excellent landscape architect and garden designer, like Piranesi, whom he knew, became so enamored of the classical ruins of Italy that he drew and painted them constantly. In the 1750s Fragonard and Robert went to Italy, staying for a time in the Villa d'Este at Tivoli as well as at the French Academy in Rome. Both left a considerable group of drawings made at this time which are among the most charming as well as the most accomplished works in the medium. Together they represent, in their voluminous work, the last breath of the spirit of the eighteenth century.

Facts About the East Building Project

Afterword by the Architect
of the East Building

The project of the East Building of the National Gallery presented a singular challenge as its location on the great Mall possesses a special significance to me. I was seventeen when I first came to America, so I felt most seriously the national and symbolic character of my task, which I faced, therefore, with both anxiety and exhilaration.

I was grateful for the opportunity this commission gave me, but felt the burden of conceiving what must be the final physical enlargement of the National Gallery. I knew it had to have the flexibility to provide a place for varied exhibitions, and, more than that, to create a welcome and exciting public space in which people could celebrate the visual arts with relaxation, stimulation and enjoyment. But most of all, I knew it had to be designed to serve an unknown future to which we look with great hope.

I. M. Pei

Site	8.88 acres (boundaries: Pennsylvania Avenue, Third Street, Madison Drive and the east end of the West Building)
Area of Total Project	604,000 square feet *East Building* 450,000 square feet *Connecting Link* 154,000 square feet *Plaza* (above Connecting Link, including paving and landscaping) 76,000 square feet
Architect	I. M. Pei & Partners, New York

The Site. The location and shape of the site posed several challenges. It was the last major undeveloped site on Pennsylvania Avenue, the inaugural route between the Capitol and The White House. This meant at the beginning that any building constructed there would have to be of significant monumental scale. Any building on the plot also had to abide by set-back lines established by the National Capital Planning Commission, as well as to observe the established heights of the cornice lines of both the Avenue and the Mall buildings, which are at substantially different levels, and at the same time relate in scale, materials and placement to the Gallery's West Building. Finally, the structure had to be appropriate to its setting and simultaneously maintain a human scale so necessary for the enjoyment of works of art.

The design solutions unfolded with a simple diagonal subdivision of the available trapezoidal space into two triangles—a larger isosceles triangle, its base facing the West Building and its exposed side bounded by Pennsylvania Avenue, and a right triangle, the base of which faces the Capitol and the exposed side of which is bounded by the Mall. A third triangle, a faceted glass roof, ties these primary elements together. The proportion of base to side in all isosceles triangles in the building, from the main skylight to the marble paving tiles, is one to one and a half.

Although the center of the site lies to the south of the powerful central east-west axis of the West Building, the towers of the East Building are designed to continue that axis and conform to the symmetry of the West Building's Fourth Street façade.

The Exhibition Areas (opening June 1, 1978). The isosceles triangle, the larger of the East Building's two major areas, provides the space for exhibition galleries and for public services. It is composed of three towers of galleries—one tower at each of the triangle's points—connected by bridges of galleries. The four main levels of this part of the building contain space for the Gallery's growing permanent collection and for temporary exhibitions, two auditoriums, a central orientation courtyard and public-service areas. The mass of this triangle is carved out and penetrated by natural light, not only from overhead—similar to the daylit courts in the West

Building—but also from the side, both symbolically and visually opening up the building to the public. The height of the towers retains and anchors the cornice line of the buildings on the south side of Pennsylvania Avenue.

The Center for Advanced Study in the Visual Arts (opening at a later date). Unlike the larger, isosceles triangle with its dramatic open spaces for works of art and flow of visitors, this right-triangle structure is subdivided into eight levels of offices for the Gallery's curatorial staff, administrative personnel, and Center for Advanced Study in the Visual Arts. A six-story library with an open reading room serves as a functional, symbolic, and visual focal point for the Center.

The Connecting Link (completed and opened June 1976). The Connecting Link joins the East Building and the West Building in an all-weather underground route. The Concourse or public area of the Connecting Link houses a 700-seat Café/Buffet and a publication sales area. The focal point in these public areas is a waterfall from the fountain on the Plaza. On the Plaza

above the Connecting Link, seven glass tetrahedrons serve as skylights for the Café below. Offices, storage, and work areas fill two levels of space adjacent to and below the public areas. The roof of this two-story, 154,000-square-foot facility serves as the granite-paved National Gallery Plaza, visually as well as functionally linking the East and West Buildings.

Construction Features

The East Building

Foundation—37 feet below grade; heavy foundation mat (6 feet thick), tie-down anchors and special waterproofing to resist the high water-table pressure. Several years of pumping ground water during construction.

Superstructure—heavy-loading, long-span design permits heavy sculpture in any gallery and provides spatial flexibility and ease of circulation. Total weight of three major steel trusses: 540 tons, the largest of which is 180 feet long, weighing 242 tons (Pennsylvania Avenue side).

Marble—the same Tennessee pink marble used in the West Building; exterior blocks 3 inches thick, cut approximately 2 feet by 5 feet. Marble blocks hung on stainless steel supports from concrete and brick core wall averaging 12 inches thick. "Solid" corner pieces. Neoprene strips between blocks allow for expansion and contraction while eliminating expansion joints as well as caulking and pointing maintenance.

Concrete— architectural concrete composed of white cement, a coarse pink aggregate, a fine white aggregate, and marble dust from the Tennessee quarries. Extensive post-tensioning. The two largest poured-concrete beams, each extending approximately 200 feet, form soffits on the north and south sides of the building. Coffered ceilings were made in forms of clear-grained fir crafted by cabinetmakers and joined and reinforced to ensure strength and precise surfaces. Low maintenance.

Space Frame/Main Skylight—225 feet long on two sides, 150 feet long on the other, spanning 16,000 square feet—more than a third of an acre —80 feet above Concourse level; constructed of a 500-ton welded steel frame, aluminum and double-pane insulating glass, including laminated safety glass and special ultra-violet filters for art preservation. Aluminum sunscreen filters direct sunlight. Each tetrahedron in the main skylight is 30 feet by 45 feet. Space frame has built-in overhead electrical outlets for lighting works of art. Neoprene gutter system carries water run-off into regular plumbing system. Electrical heating system melts snow.

Windows—double-pane insulating glass 1¼ inches thick with ½ inch of internal air space; individual panes up to 14 feet high and 105 square feet in area.

Gallery Skylights—in three top tower galleries, spanning a total of 8,600 square feet; double-pane insulating safety glass with ultra-violet filters; artificial and natural light combined; "laylight" ceilings below the skylights, with electrical grids.

Ceiling Heights—a wide range for all foreseeable installation requirements; ceilings for initial installation vary from 10 feet to 35 feet in height.

Air Outlets—modular integrated air outlets in gallery ceilings, to minimize costs of exhibition alterations and provide flexibility of gallery subdivision.

Lighting Tracks—modular grid above gallery ceilings, to minimize costs of exhibition alterations and provide flexibility of gallery subdivision.

Gallery Walls—special plywood backing, faced with wallboard, to allow maximum installation flexibility.

Gallery Floors—modular grid of electrical outlets for installation flexibility.

Elevators—8. The largest is a special 18,000-pound capacity passenger/service elevator serving all main levels; can carry objects up to 18 feet long; 10-foot ceiling.

Emergency Electrical Power—in addition to regular power, an 800kw emergency stand-by generator; automatic starting in event of power failure; provides lighting for egress from all areas, including stair and exit lights; power to operate one elevator at a time to ground-level landing and to continue operation of all alarm, security and communications systems.

Security and Fire Protection—computerized security systems for both buildings united, with one control room, including intrusion alarms, watch patrol stations, emergency communication stations, closed-circuit TV systems.

Air Conditioning Systems—systems for East Building and art-storage areas in Connecting Link consist of air filters, preheat coils, high-efficiency air washers (water spray), and reheat coils. (Other areas have cooling coils in lieu of air washers.) Systems have pre-filters and high-efficiency main filters.

Temperature and Humidity Controls—automatic; temperature and humidity sensors dispersed throughout each system and controlled from a local control panel for each unit. Remote indicating panel in Central Engineer's office, with recording instruments; alarm systems to signal all variations from optimum conditions and malfunctions; temperature control accuracy to be within plus or minus 2°F and relative humidity within plus or minus 2% from optimum conditions.

Reading Room—in Study Center Library, 72 feet high.

Offices—10-foot ceilings, 8 levels, in Study Center.

Book Stacks—9 levels, with capacity to house 350,000 volumes, allowing for expansion of the Library. Future additional book-storage capacity underground.

Study Center Interior—integrated modular double-floor construction; air circulation and electrical grid permitting rearrangement of partitions.

The Connecting Link and Plaza

Foundation—heavy foundation (concrete mat 5 feet thick) 28 feet below grade, with tie-down anchors, special waterproofing and heavy walls to resist high water-table pressure.

Construction—carried out in two stages to continue traffic on Fourth Street; required rerouting, maintaining and reconstructing major utilities, including sewer, water, telephone and high-voltage electric conduits, and building, maintaining and removing a full detour road for Fourth Street. Several years of pumping ground water during construction.

Truck Dock—long-span underground structure for trailer-truck maneuvering.

Kitchen—major facility constructed for the 700-seat Café/Buffet, which has already served more than a million visitors since June 1976. Kitchen exhausts deodorized by carbon filters.

Moving Walkway—constructed in the underground passage between the East Building and the Concourse to assist visitors as they move between the two buildings; 172 feet long.

Elevators—3, one of which is connected by underground passage to truck dock and West Building freight elevator.

Roof—a waterproofed surface with "Belgian block" granite cobble-paving and dense landscaping; also required a heavy superstructure capable of bearing full bus and truck loads along Fourth Street and throughout the Plaza area.

Fountain—52 feet long; 24 water jets with height determinable by automated wind sensor.

Waterfall—from base of fountain to Connecting Link level; 37½ feet long; 13 feet, 2 inches, top to bottom.

Plaza Sculpture/Skylights—7 tetrahedrons on Plaza, serving as skylights for Café; heights range from 11 feet, 3 inches to 6 feet, 3 inches. Reflective safety glass.

Alterations and Interconnection with West Building

New Lobby—required excavation under West Building's foundations and involved extensive structural demolition and reconstruction underneath and inside the building, including major stone remodelling in the Fourth Street lobby. New balcony on West Building's main floor and new glass wall and door in Fourth Street entrance completes visual axis of the buildings. Lobby also has new escalators, elevators and stairs to Connecting Link level.

Moat Walls—existing marble moat walls around the West Building's northeast and southeast corners maintained intact during construction of new ramp and truck dock facility, which required underpinning and reconstruction of support for moat walls.

Temporary Truck Dock—built at southeast end of West Building for uninterrupted Gallery operation.

New Refrigeration Plant—inside the west basement of the West Building, with construction of a floating steel floor support system. Excavation and reconstruction approximately 750 feet along the Gallery's Constitution Avenue frontage to install underground chilled water and steam lines connecting the plant to the East Building. Two new electrically driven, 1,250-ton capacity centrifugal chillers installed in West Building basement, cross-connected with four existing machines, for operating efficiency and flexibility. Deliver chilled water at 42°F; pumps, cross-connecting with existing pumps, send chilled water to East Building and Connecting Link, to each air-handling system.

After use in new systems, collected in major sump pits and pumped back to plant.

Condenser water cooling the refrigeration machines comes from Federally maintained gravity pipeline from Potomac River tidal basin (shared with other Federal buildings along Constitution Avenue), and returns to the river via storm sewer systems.

Energy Conservation and Economy

Heating and Cooling Systems—automated, computerized heating and air-conditioning control systems interconnecting the East and West Buildings. When outdoor air temperature is suitable, heating or cooling can be done by switching to 100% use of outside air (needing only filtering and humidity treatment). Kitchen area supplied with make-up air from Café/Buffet; garage supply ventilation is air transferred from other spaces. Heating supplied by Federal steam supply.

Windows—double-pane insulating glass minimizing the cost of heating and cooling operations while maintaining the necessary interior climate for the works of art.

Sunscreen—metal tubular grid filters out a minimum of 60% of direct sunlight; developed in full-scale mock-up tests in Florida and on the roof of the building.

Exterior Wall Construction—insulated exterior wall construction minimizing heating and cooling operations and maintaining the special interior climate.

Provisions for the Handicapped

Access—to every level, via elevators and ramps, including marble ramp at main entrance; levelator at entrance to Concourse exhibition area.

Telephone Booths and *Drinking Fountains*—special construction in certain locations.

Restroom Facilities—special construction of certain facilities.

Gallery Building Committee

Paul Mellon, chairman
Stoddard M. Stevens, John R. Stevenson,
John Hay Whitney for the Trustees,
and J. Carter Brown, Director

Gallery Planning Consultant

Dr. David W. Scott

Gallery Construction Manager

Hurley Offenbacher, Robert Engle

Gallery Construction Consultant

Carl A. Morse Co., Inc., New York

Builder

Chas. H. Tompkins Co., Washington, D.C.

Consultants

Foundation Mueser, Rutledge, Wentworth & Johnston, New York

Structural Weiskopf & Pickworth, New York

Mechanical and Electrical Syska & Hennessy, New York

Lighting Claude R. Engle, Washington, D.C.

Food Service Cini-Grissom Associates, Rockville, Md.

Landscaping Kiley, Tyndall, Walker, Charlotte, Vt.

Acoustical Cerami and Associates, Inc., Long Island City, N.Y.

Audio-Visual Will Szabo Associates Ltd., New Rochelle, N.Y.

Graphics Herman & Lees Associates, Cambridge, Mass.

Marble Malcolm Rice, Concord, Tenn.

Skylight/Window Wall Antoine-Heitmann & Associates, Inc., Kirkwood, Mo.

Traffic Travers Associates, Clifton, N.J.

East Building Data

Gross square footage of East Building:	450,000 s.f.
Height of East Building:	107 feet above grade
Length, along Pennsylvania Avenue:	405 feet
Length, along Fourth Street:	270 feet
Length, along Third Street:	135 feet
Length, along Madison Drive (Mall):	382 feet
Area of main skylight over central courtyard:	16,000 s.f.
Area of skylight areas over tower galleries:	8,600 s.f.
Exhibition areas and other public spaces:	110,000 s.f.
Exhibition area, Connecting Link level	20,000 s.f.
Exhibition areas and other public spaces on other levels	75,000 s.f.
Auditoriums (2, Connecting Link level)	10,000 s.f.
Terrace Café	5,000 s.f.
Center for Advanced Study in the Visual Arts and Gallery offices:	112,000 s.f.
Photo Archives, Rare Books, etc.	19,000 s.f.
Library Stacks, Office, Reading area	37,500 s.f.
Lobby Gallery, ground floor	4,500 s.f.
Curatorial, Administrative and Gallery Service offices	42,500 s.f.
Education and Extension Service offices	8,500 s.f.

Connecting Link Data

Gross square footage of Connecting Link:	154,000 s.f.
Café/Buffet	32,000 s.f.
Print/book sales; Extension Service	14,500 s.f.
Art storage; general storage	19,000 s.f.
Parking (110 cars); truck service dock	43,000 s.f.
Gallery offices, workshops and services	20,500 s.f.

Plaza Data

Granite-paved Plaza, including Fourth Street area:	48,000 s.f.
Plaza fountain, line of 24 water jets:	52 feet long
(Height of jets determinable by automated wind sensor)	
Waterfall at base of fountain:	37½ feet long; 13 feet, 2 inches, top to bottom
Glass tetrahedrons:	7, ranging in height from 11 feet, 3 inches to 6 feet, 3 inches

Landscaping Data

New landscaping (areas north and south of paved Plaza, north, east and south of the East Building):	92,000 s.f.
Number of new trees north of the East Building:	36
Number of new trees east and south of the East Building: (Planting to be completed during spring 1978)	61
Number of new trees north and south of the Plaza:	154

Varieties of trees and shrubs north and south of the Plaza:

Honey Locust *(Gleditsia triacanthos inermis)*
Red Oak *(Quercus borealis)*
American Holly *(Ilex opaca)*
Saucer Magnolia *(Magnolia soulangeana)*
Pink Azales *(Rhododendron "Hinodegiri")*
Red Azalea *(Rhododendron "apple blossom")*
English Boxwood *(Buxus sempervirens "Kingsville Dwarf")*

Varieties of trees north, east and south of the East Building:

Willow Oak *(Quercus phellos)*
Flowering Cherry *(Prunes vedoensis)*
Pin Oak *(Quercus palustris)*

This publication was compiled and written by Richard B. K. McLanathan

Produced by the Editor's Office, National Gallery of Art, Washington

Designed by John R. Beveridge

Printing and color separations by Stephenson, Inc., Washington

Set in Linotype Bodoni Book by Harlowe Typography, Inc., Washington

Text paper Eighty pound Quintessence Dull

Cover paper One hundred pound Quintessence Gloss

Library of Congress Cataloging in Publication Data:

McLanathan, Richard B. K.
National Gallery of Art, East Building.
1. United States, National Gallery of Art.
East Building 1. Title.
N856.N27   708'.153   78-606059